Polar Lands

KINGFISHER

Kingfisher Publications Plc
New Penderel House
283–288 High Holborn
London WC1V 7HZ
www.kingfisherpub.com

First published by Kingfisher Publications Plc 2005
2 4 6 8 10 9 7 5 3 1

1TR/0505/PROSP/RNB/140MA/F

A CIP catalogue record for this book is available from the British Library.

ISBN-13: 978 0 7534 1109 4
ISBN-10: 0 7534 1109 1

Senior editor: Catherine Brereton
Designer: Joanne Brown
Cover designer: Poppy Jenkins
Illustrators: Julian Baker, Lee Gibbons
Picture manager: Cee Weston-Baker
DTP manager: Nicky Studdart
Artwork archivist: Wendy Allison
Production controller: Jessamy Oldfield
Indexer: Sheila Clewley

Printed in China

Acknowledgements

The publishers would like to thank the following for permission to reproduce their material. Every care has been taken
to trace copyright holders. However, if there have been unintentional omissions or failure to trace copyright holders,
we apologise and will, if informed, endeavour to make corrections in any future edition.
b = bottom, *c* = centre, *l* = left, *t* = top, *r* = right

Cover: Getty Imagebank; 1 Getty Lonely Planet Images; 2–3 Getty Robert Harding pictures; 4–5 Science Photo Library (SPL)/Doug Allan;
6–7 Getty Taxi; 8–9 Corbis/Tom Bean; 8 SPL/Ted Kinsman; 9 Corbis Ralph A. Clevenger; 10–11 Corbis/Rob Howard; 11*tr* Getty NGS;
11*br* Corbis/Darrell Gulin; 12–13 Darrell Gulin; 13*tr* SPL/Simon Fraser; 13*b* Corbis/Charles Mauzy; 14–15 Corbis/Dan Guravich; 14*b* Oxford
Scientific Films/Doug Allan; 15*tr* Corbis/Kennan Ward; 15*cr* Nature Picture Library/Tom Vezo; 16–17 B&C Alexander/Arctic Photos;
17*br* Corbis/Paul A. Souders; 18 Getty Imagebank; 19*tl* B&C Alexander/Arctic Photos; 19*br* Nature Picture Library/David Pike; 21*t* Corbis/Tim
Davis; 21*c* Natural History Picture Agency/Laurie Campbell, Seapics, Hawaii, USA; 24–25 B&C Alexander/Arctic Photos; 24*b* Getty Stone;
25*b* Nature Picture Library/Doc White; 26*t* Corbis W. Perry Conway; 26*b* Corbis/Dennis Johnson, Papilio; 27 B&C Alexander/Arctic Photos;
28 B&C Alexander/Arctic Photos; 29*tr* SPL/Doug Allan; 29*bl* Ardea/Edwin Mickleburgh; 30–31 B&C Alexander/Arctic Photos;
31*t* Corbis/Galen Rowell; 32 B&C Alexander/Arctic Photos; 33*tl* B&C Alexander/Arctic Photos; 33*b* B&C Alexander/Arctic Photos;
34 B&C Alexander/Arctic Photos; 35*t* B&C Alexander/Arctic Photos; 35 Alamy/Popperfoto; 36 Alamy/B&C Alexander; 37*tl* B&C Alexander/
Arctic Photos; 37–38 B&C Alexander/Arctic Photos; 38–39 B&C Alexander/Arctic Photos; 39*tl* SPL/David Vaughan; 39*b* B&C Alexander/
Arctic Photos; 40–41 Corbis/Dan Guravich; 41*t* Corbis/Wolfgang Kaehler; 41 Corbis/Tom Brakefield; 48 B&C Alexander/Arctic Photos

Commissioned photography on pages 42–47 by Andy Crawford
Thank you to models Harrison Nagle, Joley Theodoulou and Hayley Sapsford.

KFYK **Kingfisher Young Knowledge**

Polar Lands

Margaret Hynes

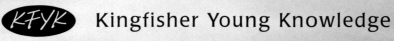

Contents

Ends of the earth

North Pole

South Pole

The polar lands are found at the opposite ends of the world, in the far north and south, around the poles. They are the coldest and windiest places on earth.

Frozen landscape

It is so cold in the polar regions that the land and sea stay frozen for most of the year. Polar animals need to be very tough to survive these conditions.

Adélie penguins

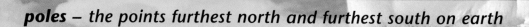

poles – *the points furthest north and furthest south on earth*

Map labels (Arctic): Alaska (USA), polar bear, RUSSIAN FEDERATION, igloo, ARCTIC OCEAN, CANADA, walrus, • North Pole, ringed seal, Arctic wolf, reindeer, Greenland, Scandinavia

Map labels (Antarctic): SOUTHERN OCEAN, SOUTHERN OCEAN, leopard seal, gentoo penguin, ANTARCTICA, South Pole •, research station, rockhopper penguin, orca, SOUTHERN OCEAN

Arctic

The Arctic surrounds the North Pole. It is made up of the Arctic Ocean and the treeless lands around it, called the tundra.

Antarctic

The Antarctic surrounds the South Pole. It is made up of a continent called Antarctica, and the Southern Ocean around it.

continent – *one of the earth's seven huge blocks of land*

Frozen features

It is so cold in the polar lands in winter that snow does not melt. Instead, it is pressed into ice as more snow falls on top of it. The ice forms thick sheets that cover the land.

Snowflakes

If you look closely at snowflakes, you will see they have many different patterns. Almost all snowflakes have six sides or six points.

melt – *change from snow or ice into water*

Underwater giants

Icebergs are massive chunks of freshwater ice that float in the polar seas. The biggest part of an iceberg lies below the surface of the water.

Crashing ice

Icebergs break off the edge of polar ice sheets and crash into the sea. This mostly happens during the summer when the ice melts a little.

freshwater – *water that is fresh, like rain or river water, not salty like seawater*

Light and dark

The polar lands are unique places. During the long, harsh winters it is dark for almost the whole day. In summer, the sun does not set for weeks on end.

Lighting the way

In the summer, the sun dips in the sky at night, but it still lights up the land. Even though it is past midnight, these people can find their way home.

unique – not like any other

Strange lights

Near the poles, the night skies are sometimes filled with glorious light shows. These spectacular natural displays are called auroras, or the northern and southern lights.

Summer squirrelling

The ground squirrel survives the winter by hibernating. In summer, it makes the most of the constant daylight to gather a store of food for the next winter.

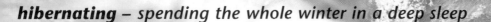

hibernating – spending the whole winter in a deep sleep

Tundra in bloom

The tundra is a cold plain that is covered with snow in winter. When the snow melts in summer, the tundra comes alive with flowers and animals.

Flowering carpet

A carpet of grasses, mosses and lichens covers the tundra in summer. These plants grow close to the ground, avoiding the freezing winds that howl above them.

plain – flat, mainly treeless area of land

Making seeds in the sun

In the short summer, tundra flowers such as this Arctic poppy quickly blossom and produce seeds. Then the seeds lie frozen in the soil all winter.

Dining alone

Lone grizzly bears roam the tundra when it is in bloom. They feed on mammals, insects and plants, getting as fat as possible before the winter, when they hibernate in a den.

blossom – *produce flowers*

Adaptable animals

Animals that spend the winter in polar lands are specially adapted to survive in freezing temperatures. Many also have white coats so that they cannot be spotted in the snowy landscape.

Anti-freeze

This Antarctic ice fish survives in waters where most other fish would freeze solid. It has special chemicals in its body that stop it from freezing.

camouflage – a shape, colour or pattern that helps hide an animal

Changing coats

In winter, the ptarmigan grows thick white feathers for extra warmth and camouflage in the snow. In spring, it turns brown.

ptarmigan – winter

ptarmigan – spring and summer

Survival of the fattest

There is no danger of this walrus getting cold. Like all sea mammals, it has a thick layer of blubber under its skin. This body fat keeps it warm.

mammals – *warm-blooded animals that feed their young on milk*

Who eats what?

Like all animals, Arctic animals keep busy finding food. Some eat plants, while others are predators. Most animals need to protect themselves from predators.

Protective parents

Musk oxen do not run away when Arctic wolves come near. Instead, the adults form a circle around their young, so the wolves cannot catch them.

predators – animals that hunt and eat other animals

Arctic food chain

Arctic wolves are the top predators in this food chain. They eat musk oxen, hares and lemmings, which in turn feed on grass and lichens.

eats

Arctic wolf

eats

musk ox   Arctic hare   lemming

eats

grass and lichens

eats

Bully bird

In Antarctica, the skua is an aggressive predator. It threatens penguins and steals their eggs.

food chain – *a diagram that shows who eats what in a particular place*

King of the ice

The polar bear is the largest and most powerful hunter of the Arctic. Bears roam alone over long distances each day in search of seals to eat. They also catch fish with their sharp claws.

Surviving the cold

Polar bears spend most of their time on ice floes. They are also excellent swimmers and can spend many hours in the freezing water. Oily fur and a layer of blubber keeps these bears warm.

roam – *wander over a large area*

Junk food

Polar bears can stray into towns to find food. Sometimes they visit rubbish dumps, where they may be poisoned or injured.

Mother care

Baby polar bears are called cubs. They are born in a warm, cosy den that their mother digs in the snow. They grow quickly on their mother's rich, fatty milk.

ice floes – large chunks of floating ice

Long-distance travel

For many polar birds and mammals, winter in the Arctic is just too cold. These animals migrate south to warmer places, and return again in spring.

Nomads of the north

Caribou are a type of deer. In winter, they live in forests on the edge of the Arctic. In summer, they travel 1,000 kilometres north to spend the summer feeding on tundra plants.

migrate – make the same journey every year at the same season

Flying visits

Arctic terns fly further than other birds. Each year they fly from the Arctic to the Antarctic and back, seeing summer at both poles.

On the hoof

Caribou can walk on deep snow without sinking. This is because their wide, fur-fringed hooves act like snowshoes by spreading their weight.

snowshoes – shoes for walking on snow, with a frame that is strapped to the foot

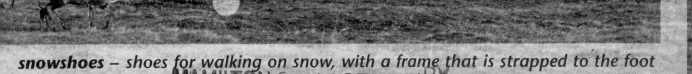

Life in polar seas

Polar seas are cold, but not as cold and hard to live in as polar lands. The deep waters of the polar seas are teeming with sea creatures.

Antarctic sea floor

Colourful anemones, fan worms and starfish sit on the Antarctic seabed. Sea slaters and sea spiders creep along the floor.

shoaling fish

sea anemone

sea slater

teeming – *full of living creatures*

Sea food

Many animals in polar seas, from tiny fish to large whales, feed on plankton. These are microscopic animals and plants that drift in the water.

fan worm

sea spiders (red and yellow)

starfish

microscopic – *much too small to be seen with the human eye*

Sea mammals

The polar seas are home to whales, seals, sea lions and walruses. These mammals have blubber to keep them warm, and streamlined bodies that help them move through the water easily.

Making a splash

Whales, such as this humpback whale, swim in the icy polar waters. They leap in the air and fall back into the water with a splash. This is called breaching.

streamlined – having a smooth body shape that moves easily through water

Changing coats

Harp seals are born with fluffy white coats. The mothers take care of their babies for about two weeks, then the pups grow grey adult coats and must look after themselves.

Tusk tools

Walruses drag themselves out of the water using their tusks as levers. They also use their tusks to dislodge shellfish on the seabed.

tusks – long teeth that poke out of an animal's mouth

albatross

Flying squad

Many sea-birds spend summer at the poles. Most live on land, flying out over the sea and diving to catch food. The albatross stays at sea for most of the time, only coming ashore to lay its eggs.

Pointy eggs

Guillemots lay their eggs on cliff ledges. The eggs are pointed at one end. If they are nudged, they spin in a circle and do not fall off the cliff.

sea-bird – *a bird that lives near the sea and feeds from the sea*

Cliff colonies

Puffins make their nests high up on cliffs so that predators cannot reach them. They breed in large, noisy groups called colonies.

breed – *produce babies*

Crowds of penguins

Penguins live in the coastal areas of the Antarctic. These birds cannot fly, but they use their wings to glide underwater as they chase their food.

Group hug

These young emperor penguins are huddling together to keep warm. They take turns to go in the middle where it is warmest.

glide – *move smoothly through the water*

Sliding along

To travel quickly on land, Adélie penguins slide over the snow on their tummies. They use their wings to push and steer.

Feet off the ground

The ice is much too cold for young chicks. To keep off it, they stand on their mum's or dad's feet and snuggle under a special flap of skin on the adult's belly.

steer – guide themselves in the right direction
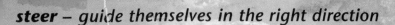

Inuit people

The Inuit people live in North America and Greenland. Traditionally, they travelled about in family groups and survived by fishing and hunting. Today, many Inuit live in towns.

Cosy icebox

When they are on hunting trips, Inuit people build igloos as temporary homes. Although they are made from frozen blocks of ice and loose snow, they are cosy and warm inside.

temporary – lasting for a short time

Boat sense

The Inuit are expert boat-builders. They cover their boats in sealskin, which keeps them watertight. This boat is an umiak.

watertight – *something that keeps water out*

32) A herder's life

Some Saami, Lapp and Chukchi people are herders. They follow wild reindeer herds and settle in camps wherever the reindeer stop to feed.

Reindeer power
Reindeer pull sleds and carry heavy loads and riders. They also provide meat, and skins for clothing and shelter.

herders – people who look after herds of animals

Winter warmth

These men are wearing warm winter coats, called parkas, made from reindeer skin. The soft, warm fur is worn against the men's skin.

Mobile homes

Arctic herders move several times a year, so their homes have to be simple and light. They live in tents made from a cone-shaped wooden frame, covered with reindeer skins.

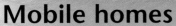

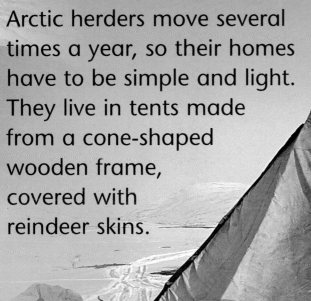

Polar exploration

Many explorers risked their lives trying to be the first people to set foot at the poles. In 1909, Robert Peary reached the North Pole. In 1911, Roald Amundsen beat Robert Scott in a race to the South Pole.

Modern-day explorers

Today's polar explorers wear layers of specially designed clothing to keep warm in freezing temperatures. They pull their supplies on lightweight sledges.

lightweight – *designed to weigh as little as possible*

An explorer's best friends

Amundsen and his team learned from Arctic people and used husky dogs to pull their sledges. Huskies are strong and intelligent, and well adapted to the cold.

Over sea and land

Scott and Amundsen sailed part of the way to the South Pole. Once they reached land, they loaded their supplies onto sledges and continued their journeys on skis.

Scott's ship, the **Terra Nova**

Modern life

Improvements in transport, food, building and clothing have brought a modern way of life to the Arctic. Most people now live in small towns and work in modern industries.

Arctic towns

Arctic towns are like other small towns, except that water has to be delivered by truck. The water would freeze if it was distributed through pipes.

People carrier

The people living in polar lands no longer rely on animals for transport. Today, they travel on skidoos or snowmobiles – motorized sledges.

industries – businesses that make goods and sell these goods for money

Oil industry

The Arctic's rich supplies of oil are processed in plants such as this one. Oil is one of the world's most important fuels and is used to make many goods. The oil industry provides jobs but harms the Arctic environment.

environment – *natural surroundings*

Scientific research

The only people who live in Antarctica are scientists working in research stations. They study Antarctica's wildlife and find out about its climate.

Weather watching

Every day, scientists measure and record the weather conditions. The measuring instruments are attached to a balloon that floats 20 kilometres above ground.

climate – usual weather conditions in one place over a period of time

Drilling for information

Using a special drill, scientists extract long samples of ice, called cores. The layers of ice have built up over thousands of years. Studying them helps scientists learn about the earth's past climate.

Animal tracking

A tag on this Weddell seal's tail helps scientists record when and where they see this particular seal. This helps us learn more about seals' lives and how to protect them.

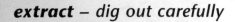

extract – *dig out carefully*

Protecting wildlife

People have lived in the Arctic for thousands of years without harming the environment. Recently, though, people have endangered wildlife by hunting and by pollution.

Free ride home

Polar bears are quite rare and most northern countries have laws to protect them. Bears that wander into towns are caught and airlifted back to the wild.

pollution – *chemicals and other materials that damage the environment*

Watching and protecting

These tourists in Antarctica are on a carefully organized trip. This helps make sure that wildlife is not disturbed too much.

Saving sea mammals

Special sanctuaries in the Southern Ocean protect the feeding grounds of whales and orcas. Most countries have agreed not to hunt in these areas.

orca (killer whale)

sanctuaries – safe places that are protected from damage by humans

Smart snowflakes

Make a paper snowflake

Real snowflakes have six sides or points, so you need to fold a piece of paper into six sections before you create a pattern.

1

Place the plate onto the white paper. Using a pencil, draw round the plate to make a circle. Then carefully cut out the circle shape.

You will need
- Plate
- White paper
- Pencil
- Scissors
- Coloured card (optional)
- Glue (optional)
- Glitter (optional)
- Shiny paper (optional)

2

Use the white paper circle you have made to create your snowflake. Start by folding the circle in half to make a semi-circle.

3

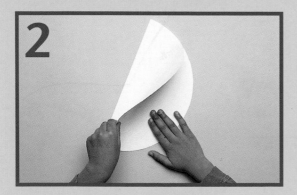

Fold the semi-circle into three equal parts, as shown, to make six sections. This means your snowflake will have six sides.

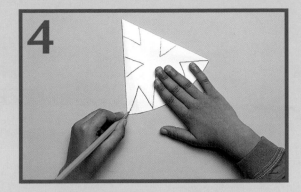

4

Draw a pattern on your folded paper. Make sure you do not draw right across the paper. You could start by copying this pattern.

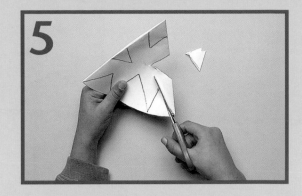

5

Cut away sections of the folded paper, following the pattern. Take care not to cut right across the width of the paper.

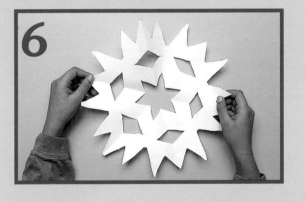

6

Unfold your snowflake carefully. You will see that the patterns on each of the six sections are identical – like a real snowflake!

Have fun making and displaying lots of snowflakes. You can glue your snowflakes onto coloured card and decorate them with glitter and shiny paper.

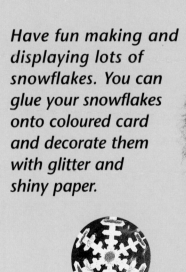

Ice fun!

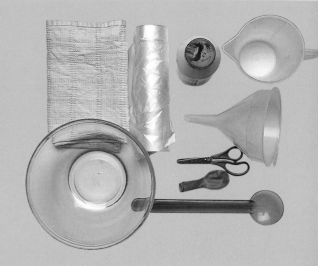

Incredible iceberg

An iceberg may take thousands of years to form, from layers and layers of snow. You can make your own iceberg overnight.

You will need
- Jug
- Water
- Balloon
- Funnel

- Plastic bag
- Freezer
- Clear bowl
- Tablespoon

- Salt
- Scissors
- Tea towel

1

Fill the jug with cold tap water. Fit the funnel into the neck of the balloon and hold it in place. Ask an adult to help you fill the balloon.

2

Ask an adult to tie the end of the balloon to seal the water inside. Put the balloon inside a plastic bag and place in a freezer overnight.

3

Next day, fill the clear bowl three-quarters full with water. Then add about 5 to 10 tablespoons of salt to make seawater.

Take the balloon out of the freezer and remove the plastic bag. Cut the end off the balloon and carefully peel it off the ice.

Using a tea towel or cloth so that your fingers do not stick to the cold ice, carefully place your iceberg in the bowl of salty water.

Your iceberg will float in the salty water. You will see that only a small portion of the whole iceberg stays above the water's surface.

Penguin game

Play the penguin game and pretend to be a penguin keeping its egg safely above the cold ice.

You will need
● Bean bag

Penguins keep their eggs and babies safely above the ice by carrying them on their feet. To play the penguin game, you and a friend need to pass a bean bag 'egg' to each other without dropping it on the floor, using only your feet.

Penguin mask

Make a penguin face

Rockhoppers are small Antarctic penguins with brightly coloured faces. Make a penguin mask and you can look like one!

Start by tracing the rockhopper penguin template at the back of this book. Then transfer your tracing onto your piece of card.

You will need
- Tracing paper
- Pencil
- Black card
- Scissors
- Moulding dough
- Apron or overall
- Paint: red, yellow
- Elastic
- Glue
- Yellow tissue paper

Using the scissors, carefully cut out the shape of the penguin mask. You may want to ask an adult to help you with this.

Use a pencil and moulding dough to pierce holes for the elastic strap and for the eyeholes. Enlarge the eyeholes with scissors.

Wearing an apron or overall, paint your penguin mask. Use red for the eyes and orange for the beak. (Make orange paint by mixing red and yellow paint.)

When the paint is dry, cut a piece of elastic that is long enough to fit around your head. Tie the ends into each of the small holes on the side of the mask.

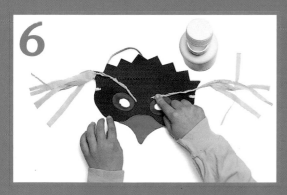

Cut two strips of yellow tissue paper. Spread a thin line of glue above the eyes, and glue on the strips of tissue paper to make the penguin's feathery eyebrows.

Have fun wearing your mask and pretending to be a rockhopper penguin.

Index

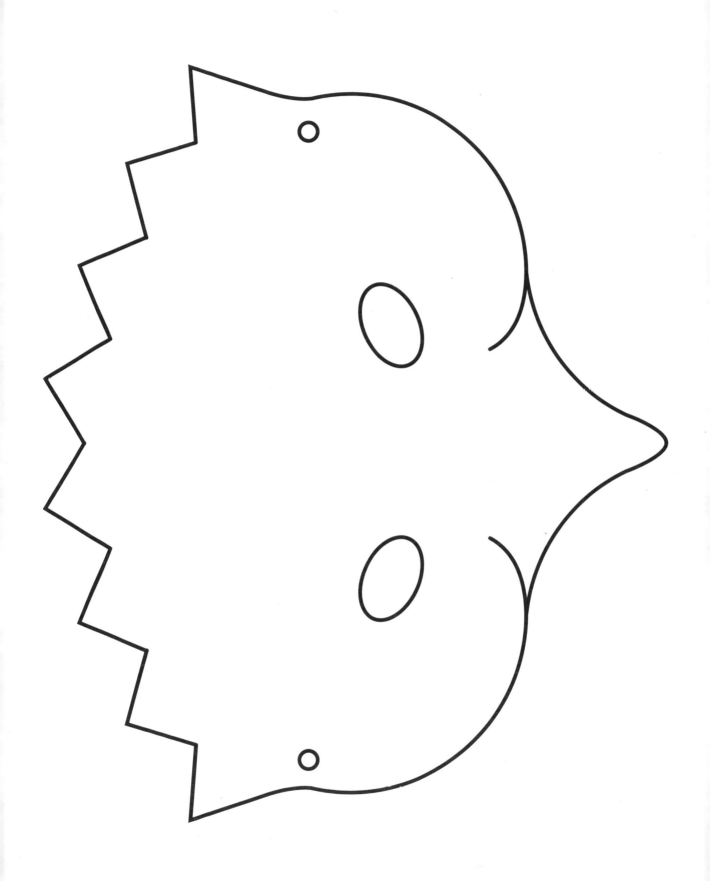